The World of African Song

THE WORLD of African SONG

Miriam Makeba

Music Edited by Jonas Gwangwa
and E. John Miller, Jr.
Introduction and Notes by
Solomon Mbabi-Katana
Illustrations by Dean Alexander

Quadrangle Books   Chicago   1971

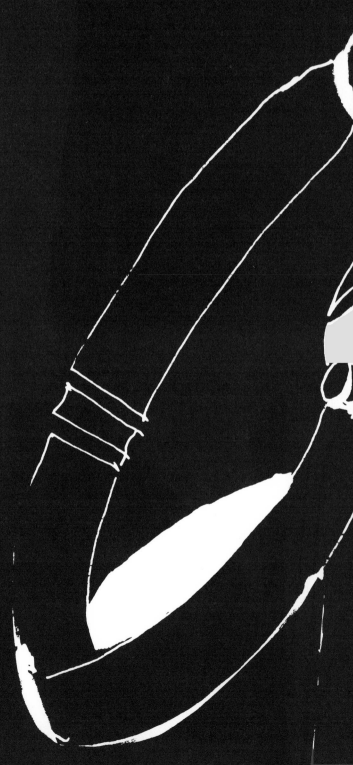

Library of Congress Catalog Card Number:
65–18247

All songs are used by permission of Makeba
Music, Inc.

SBN Cloth 8129-0138-X
SBN Paper 8129-6119-6

Preface

One of the most rewarding challenges for the musician is the assimilation of songs from other lands. Whether he is a concert performer or a fireside strummer, musical enrichment results not only from technique but from a varied repertoire. Most musicians perform songs from cultures other than their own, both because of their appreciation for the music of these societies and because of the intrinsic pleasure it affords the performers themselves and their audiences.

Folk musicians have for years relished material from other cultures, and recently certain styles, notably the Latin American, have been gaining audiences within the popular music idiom. Not often, however, has the music of Africa found popularity. With the notable exception of "Mbube" [also known as "Wimoweh," or "The Lion Sleeps Tonight"], African music is relatively unknown.

Fortunately, some of us have been exposed to Miriam Makeba. This book will introduce others to an enchanting new musical experience: the experience of African song.

5

CONTENTS

The World of African Song

Introduction

From earliest times Westerners have been awed and fascinated by Africa's unique music. About 500 B.C., when Hanno the Carthaginian returned from West Africa, he wrote that upon landing on an island off the coast he and his companions had seen many fires being kindled by night and had heard "the noise of pipes and cymbals and a din of tom-toms and the shouts of a multitude." They were frightened and hastily left at the urging of their interpreters. Some two thousand years later, in the early 1620's, Richard Jobson, sent among the Mandingoes of West Africa by the Merchant Adventurers of London, reported how alien the sound of African music had been to him. In the Mandingo King's house, he said, "his drummes, the onely instruments of warre which we see amongst them," hung by his chair. "Neither," he continued, "are these drummes without dayly imployment, for this is their continuall custome every night after it seemes they have filled their bellies, they repaire to this Court of Guard, making fires both in the middle of the house, and in the open yard, about which they do continue drumming, hooping, singing, and making a hethenish noyse, most commonly until the day beginnes to breake, when as we conceive dead-sleepes take them." Some believed that the noise was made "to feare and keep away the Lyons, and ravening beasts," and pointed out that virtually no village was "without such poore drums they use," and if one was without drums then "they continue the custome, through hooping, singing, and using their voyces, but when it happens musicke is amongst them, then is the horrible din."

We have learned much about Africa since Jobson's day—much, that is, of Africa's geography, economics, and politics. Culturally, however, the divide, while narrowed, is still largely unbridged. The songs in this book are therefore doubly welcome, for apart from their intrinsic interest and beauty they introduce us to aspects of African culture in Southern Africa still widely unknown to us.

Most of the songs presented here are the songs of the Zulu and Xhosa peoples. Both the Xhosa and Zulu languages, like those of all the Bantu peoples, are musically accented, abounding in rich vowel sounds which lend themselves to song. Both languages also have a wide range of consonants, including the famous "click sounds,"

which we shall explain later. In this book the songs have been provided with musical accompaniment of triadic chords based on seventeenth-century European harmony, which enables us to appreciate and assimilate sounds that would otherwise appear too unfamiliar. Melodically, most of the songs in this book are distinguished by a wide use of syncopated rhythms. Syncopated rhythm, though a common feature in African music, is not used as extensively as in American jazz music. In fact, the peculiarities in the use of syncopated rhythm are a major difference between the two types of music.

The songs are direct transcriptions of performances of African folk songs; although they represent the interpretation of one particular African artist, each is nonetheless authentic. Other transcriptions would, of course, result in different versions. But folk music is music created by a people, and not by an individual composer, and thus it lends itself to different moods, different emphases, different circumstances—and is, finally, as variable as life itself.

Miriam Makeba adds yet another element to her interpretation. The songs she sings are songs that have usually remained unwritten. They have been transmitted by a long line of African singers, each one of whom invests them with his or her own personality. Miss Makeba brings her own unique interpretation to her material—an interpretation that differs from that of most of her predecessors, not only because she has assimilated the particular experience of city life in South Africa [which in itself is a new mutation of the folk experience], but because, far more than most African singers, she has been exposed to musical influences that are largely non-African. Since her "discovery" by a movie producer who directed the social protest film *Come Back Africa,* her life has differed from that of most black South African artists. She has gained a degree of freedom they can only hope for. She has lived in the United States where she has been acclaimed by vast audiences of blacks and whites. And she has sung to African audiences, and in her travels across the continent has learned firsthand many of the variations of Africa's music found in lands other than her own South Africa. All this has broadened her understanding as an artist and enriched her singing. As those who have heard her know, her style is marked by a strong, dynamic, and huskily compelling quality which is quite distinct and unforgettable.

Before looking at the songs themselves, we may do well to consider the historical background of African music as well as some of the types of musical instruments and song styles of Africa.

The Historical Background

In the distant past what we now call the black African peoples inhabited not only Africa but also other regions. They were spread in a great arc, or semi-circle, which swung from East and Northeast Africa up to an apex in Southern India and Ceylon, before swinging south again across the Indonesian archipelago and into Australasia. The migrations of peoples throughout history largely erased the top of the arc and fragmented the rest. But traces of the original black-skinned race are still to be found in Southern India and in parts of the Pacific, as well as in Australia and the islands of Oceania, even though it is in Africa that the main body of the race has made its homeland.

There is thus a reason for the many similarities between black Africa and Indonesia. That species of coastal palm tree which is regarded as so peculiarly African is the same as that found in Indonesia, where scientists believe it originated. As with peoples and plants, so with music. The late ethnomusicologist Curt Sachs commented that, in Uganda, one of the Ganda peoples "divide the octave into five, in principle equal, steps of around 240 cents, which corresponds to the *salendro* gender of Java's and Bali's *gamelan* orchestras." The Bapende and Chopi peoples of Southern Africa, he also observed, give their xylophones an "arrangement with even steps of about 171 cents in an octave, which amounts exactly to the current genders of Siam and Burma" —a striking coincidence, if coincidence it is.

Yet another hint of a relationship between Indonesia and Africa is provided by the drum. Today, of all instruments, it is regarded as the most characteristically African of all musical instruments. In his essay on the origin of African civilizations, the German anthropologist Leo Frobenius wrote as early as 1898 that, "By far the larger part of African drums consist of a log

scooped out, one or both ends covered with hide. I do no more than state the fact that the Indonesian method of bracing drums reappears on the West African coast."

The next significant influence in African music was the Arab invasion of Northern Africa in the seventh century. Though strongest in North and West Africa, and down the East African coast, the Arabic influence has nevertheless penetrated as far into the heartland of the continent as Rwanda-Burundi.

Beyond any doubt the European influence of more recent times has been of major significance in today's African music. Yet a close comparison between African and European music raises doubts as to whether *all* the similarities with European music stem from recent contact. Strong similarities, for example, are found between European and African folk music, both of which share diatonic and pentatonic scales, certain kinds of polyphony, and other characteristics.

The Musical Instruments of Africa
Normally the African folk songs in this book are accompanied by hand clapping, but drums or other traditional African instruments may join in the accompaniment. As the popular impression is that the drum, and the drum alone, is Africa's musical instrument, we may consider what instrumentation has, in fact, been in use on the continent.

Curt Sachs and Erich von Hornbostel—the latter also an ethnomusicologist—divided instruments into four types: idiophones, or instruments whose bodies vibrate to create sound; membranophones, or instruments with a vibrating membrane; aerophones, or instruments that permit a column of air to vibrate within themselves; and chordophones, which have vibrating strings. Log drums, bells, and rattles would thus be classed as idiophones; skin drums, with a single or double drumhead, as membranophones; trumpets, horns, and flutes as aerophones; and harps, lutes, zithers, and bows as chordophones.

As we have indicated, it is above all the membranophonic skin drum that has, from early times, always appeared to Westerners as the most characteristic African instrument, perhaps on account of the skill with which African

musicians have handled it. In fact, however, the birthplace of the drum is unknown. Whereas some instruments appear to have emerged, or have been discovered, independently in various places, the skin drum is believed by ethnomusicologists to have originated in one place. The fact that that it is found well-nigh everywhere is taken as evidence that it was one of the earliest instruments known to man.

Skin drums, in Africa, are usually beaten either with the hand [using only the fingers, or the fingers, the fist, and the palm] or with a curved stick. Frequently drummers form a "drum choir," each taking different parts. A typical Ghanaian drum is the *gangan* or *dundun* drum, which is shaped like an hourglass, the membranes at each end being joined to each other by numerous strings. In this way it is possible for the drummer to vary the pitch by holding the drum under his arm and squeezing it with his elbow, thus tightening the drumheads. Drum music of great variation can thus be created even by a single drummer, beating the drum as he walks or dances along. Drumming, however, has reached its greatest complexity in Western Africa, while in Eastern and Southern Africa the drum is more likely to be supplemented by other instruments.

The open grazing lands and wide treeless plains of South Africa have conditioned the music of the South African people in various ways. The absence of forests and thick vegetation has made the thick hollow logs necessary for typical African drums—which are found in the Congo forests or in West Africa—hard to come by. Hence South African drums are of a different type. Among the Khoi Khoi, or Hottentots, the drum is customarily made of a pot or a calabash over which a skin is stretched. Among the Xhosa of the Transkei, a dried ox hide is fastened to poles planted in the earth, so that the surface of the hide is about three feet from the ground. The upper surface of the hide thus forms a drum, upon which the musicians play with beaters engraved with ornaments. The Venda, Pedi, Tswana, and Sotho peoples of the same region construct their drums from a conical resonator of any material—usually soft wood—covered with a hide pegged into the drum while wet, with hide strips afterward being laced between the pegs.

One other element distinguishes the music of Southern Africa: women, too, are often allowed to play the drums. In other parts of Africa this is generally unthinkable, the traditional role of the women being to clap their hands rhythmically in accompaniment to the music, or else to provide a chorus or counterpoint.

African drum lore is quite variegated. In some parts of the continent certain drums are regarded as being of divine origin, and their sound is identified with the voices of the gods themselves. Elsewhere the drum is a symbol of power. Certain drums can be beaten only when war is declared. In Rwanda, among the Watusi, only the Mwami, the traditional ruler, or else the Queen Mother, is allowed to possess a set of drums. Among some peoples drummers have particularly high status, the drummer's skill being passed on from father to son after arduous training. The long hours of ceaseless repetition, with never the slightest mistake being overlooked, are evidence of the importance of drum music, which is also reflected in the magnificent decorations of some drums. These take the form of elaborate carvings, bead decorations, or embellishment with the skins of zebras or other striking animals. In Southern Africa, however, in recent times, drummakers, without suitable wood to hand, have had to use the debris of modern technology—jettisoned gasoline cans, oil drums, and similar improvisations.

Among idiophones, rattles, clappers, and bells are widely used. Although the xylophone came originally from Indonesia, it has by now also become strongly identified with Africa, where it is found from the Indian Ocean to the Atlantic. In South Africa, as well as further north, xylophone ensembles are not uncommon, being composed of anything from a trio [treble, alto, and bass] in South Africa to a xylophonic quintet in Equatorial Africa, and larger groupings in Western Africa and Southern Mozambique. The xylophones vary greatly in complexity, some being relatively simple instruments made of slats laid across two felled trees, whereas in others, supported on a wooden frame, resonating gourds hang below each bar. In the Southern Congo the Luba people play *malimbe* xylophones which are paired together in male and female forms—the male xylophone having sixteen bars, and the female

nine. Some xylophones are small enough to be portable, being suspended from the player's neck by a cord so that he can make music during a procession, or, together with other musicians, as part of a "minstrel" orchestra.

Related to the xylophone is the "sansa," or thumb piano, which is also found throughout the continent. Under different names it appears throughout West, East, and South Africa. It clearly originated on the continent, since it is found nowhere else in the world, except where peoples of African descent have taken it, i.e., mainly in the Americas. In South Africa, in the wooded areas of the Northeast, it is widely used by the Venda and the Chopi. The "sansa" consists of a number of metal tongues attached to a sounding box that is usually rectangular, although it also appears in other shapes. Individual tongues of the instrument are struck by the player to produce a sound which, like that of the xylophone, is soft, but whose tone somewhat resembles that of a plucked instrument.

Flutes, horns, trumpets, ocarinas, and panpipes —all aerophones—are found all over Africa, and can quite appropriately be used to accompany the songs in this book.

Musical bows are also common throughout Africa, and are even pictured in the ancient rock paintings found in the Sahara. In South Africa itself bows are almost the only chordophones known. Usually the bow is designed exclusively as a musical instrument, although in earlier times some hunters—for example, the Abathwa [Bushmen] in the Kalahari Desert—used their bows both as weapons and as musical instruments. In the absence of materials to resonate the feeble string sound emitted by the shooting bow, the hunter's mouth serves the purpose adequately. When the string is plucked, it produces a fundamental note which persists as a drone throughout the melody. By changing the shape of the mouth over the persistent drone of the fundamental, the musician-hunter can sound different harmonic series needed for his melody. Farther north other chordophones are found, such as the zither. In East Africa and the Nilotic Sudan, for example, lyres, known as "kissars," are used. The body of the "kissar" is often made of a gourd, or a turtle shell, and in earlier times, during the tribal wars, even the skulls of slain enemies were used for this purpose. Arched harps and zithers are also used in these regions, while in areas that have been subjected to Arab acculturation, lutes are found. But in South Africa, from where our songs are drawn, the bow is, as we have said, virtually the only chordophone in common use.

The Role of Music in African Life

In Africa, music has always been more directly related to daily life than in Europe. European children are usually taught songs from fairy tales or from history, whereas the songs of African children more often deal with the familiar and immediate—with the lagoon they know, with poverty, or with the circumstances of birth. Only when it comes to songs connected with the games they play do African and European children share a common theme.

It is, then, from music that the African child mainly learns about life. Whether it is—as in this book—a song about a wayside medicine man, a song to encourage warriors going into battle, a love song, or a lament, the African song is usually drawn from and related to everyday life. Work songs, boating songs, puberty rite songs, marching songs, cowherding songs, harvest songs, drinking songs, hunting songs, war songs, funeral dirges, ceremonial songs, wedding songs, cradle songs, ritual songs—in every instance music and song are interwoven with African life. One has only to hear the song of reapers mowing grass to the sound of a flute, a bagpipe in the West African savannah lands, the song of paddlers on an African river, or the thunder of drums and the joyful chorus of voices at an African dance deep in the night to realize the pervasive quality of music in African culture. Even communication becomes fused with music, as in the sonorous sounds of the famous "talking drums" of Cameroon, Nigeria, Ghana, and elsewhere, which tap and roll out their speech symbols from valley to valley and through the forest groves.

As all over Africa, the folk song in South Africa is a repository of poetry, history, ballads, epics, and stories of all kinds. The folk song recalls historical events such as wars, famines, severe droughts, epidemics, coronations, and

weddings. The song "Mayibuye" in this book is a notable example of a song depicting incidents of historic interest. It is a Xhosa patrotic song intended to inspire the oppressed African people of South Africa by reminding them of their past glories.

Varied as they are, the songs in this book may be broadly classified in three main groups:

(1) Genuine traditional songs
(2) Folk songs of recent origin
(3) Songs composed by modern African song writers

The notes accompanying each song suggest the category in which they belong.

Among the traditional songs are those which strive to teach the ancient African ideals of physical fitness and bravery—ideals that reached their greatest influence during the days when Shaka Zulu welded together the great Zulu nation out of many disparate tribal groups. A song which seeks to instill courage is "Jikele' Maweni." It describes dances and sham fights among the Xhosa youth of South Africa.

Other songs provide an accepted way to criticize the rule of tyrants or despotic chiefs—a means of airing grievances that was permitted not only by the Zulu, Xhosa, Venda, and Tsonga of South Africa, but also by the Nyoro and Ganda of Uganda, and the Watusi of Rwanda and Burundi. This freedom of expression also finds an echo in the tolerance accorded not only to the sayings but also to the doings of the "griots" of West Africa. [The "griot"—minstrel, buffoon, and magician in one—while of low social status, had the right to mock and insult anybody and to indulge in behavior punishable in others.]

The New African Music

With the coming of the white man, and more particularly with the growth of towns and cities in Southern Africa, African song underwent a transformation to what has been called "neo-folk music." "It was about the year 1940," writes A. M. Jones, author of *Studies in African Music,* "that we in Northern Rhodesia became aware that a new sort of music was coming into the country, though it had been generating elsewhere decades before that. It quickly captivated the young

Africans in schools and the young men and women in mine and town compounds . . ." Originally of South African origin—as was clear from the fact that the words of the new songs were usually in Sindebele—the music quickly became acclimatized in the Central African region. Before long the new style had spread to both East and West Africa, where it is mainly known as "High Life." At once completely African and completely modern, it represents a new departure in folk music—an adaptation, in effect, of African culture to urban life. As a neo-folk tradition it is now deeply rooted across the African continent and has virtually displaced the more traditional African forms, just as in Europe the old medieval folk songs have been displaced by "popular" music. "It seems," to quote A. M. Jones again, "as if for some unknown reason the impact of American jazz and Western four-part harmony have suddenly produced more or less all over Africa a simultaneous urge to create the same sort of derivative music." Among the songs in this book one may note "Into Yam," "Langa More," and "Thanayi," which have grown out of urban South Africa and combine both non-African and African elements. A characteristic of such songs is the so-called "Umbagonga" rhythm, which possesses jazz elements. The songs can be heard at Gumba-Gumba African parties in the cities of South Africa— "night club" parties completely alien to the traditions of African village life.

A few songs in this book, usually those with political overtones arising from the tragic racial conflict that divides the peoples of South Africa today, have been composed by modern South African songwriters. One of these songs, "Ntyilo-Ntyilo," paradoxically contrasts phrases of lamentation over the "doomed land of South Africa" with a jubilant melody. "Magwalandini" ["You Cowards"] is a brave man's exhortation to his countrymen to awake, rise up from their shameful torpor, and regain their dignity. What the song lacks in text is made up for by its tune, which is reminiscent of the traditional Zulu warrior songs. Melodically wistful, on the other hand, is the song, "Cameroon," which, by implication, contrasts the peace and freedom of that presumably idyllic land with the harsh racial confrontation that has become the main fact of life in South Africa today.

Among the traditional songs in this book are songs that are sung purely for entertainment on social occasions. One such song is "Qongqothwane," or the "Click Song," as it is usually known, which has been made famous by Miriam Makeba's recordings. Patriotic songs such as "Zenizenabo" and "Amampondo," which begin with simple swinging melodies, become rhythmically broken toward the end. This is a common technique in African music. As most African songs are accompanied by dancing, African music usually starts with simple rhythms which gradually, as in the normal dance pattern, build to a complexity toward the climactic end.

Story songs such as "Dubula" and "Ngoma Kurila" are sung while telling a tale, and they are typical of African fireplace entertainment of young family members by their elders. Sometimes such songs do not merely appear in the middle of a story as a diversion. They may be sung stories, such as "Dubula," or they may be ballads, in which case they tend to be technically difficult.

African music abounds in love songs with simple lyrical texts, such as "Woza," "Into Yam," and "Nomthini." They are innocently outspoken and honest, suffused with a passionate restraint that is typically African.

As we have said, the language of the Bantu people of South Africa is musically accented. It includes the "click sounds" c, q, and x, and the lateral sounds dl and hl. Such consonants occur frequently in the songs in this book, with the exception of the c click, which appears more rarely—as in the songs "Mayibuye," "Into Yam," and "Cameroon."

In order to pronounce c in the languages of the Bantu people, place the tip of the tongue against the ridge of the palate just behind the teeth. Press hard, and release it suddenly.

The letter x appears frequently in the following songs: "Jikele' Maweni," "Thanayi," "Olilili," "Mayibuye," and "Magwalandini." To produce x, place the end of the tongue flat against the palate, with the tip lying behind the teeth, and then release the tongue suddenly.

The letter q appears frequently in the "Click Song," in "Qhude," in "Mayibuye," in "Zenizenabo," and in "Umqokozo." The shape to be assumed by the sound passage while pronouncing this letter is given in the description of "Qongqothwane," or the "Click Song."

The lateral hl has been used extensively in the following songs: "Nomeva," "Ntyilo-Ntyilo," "Thanayi," "Woza," "Mayibuye," "Nomthini," "Ngoma Kurila," and "Khuluma." In pronouncing this lateral, the rim of the tongue is placed against the ridge of the palate, leaving two slight openings on each side of the tongue, with air being breathed out through the openings.

The lateral dl appears in "Langa More" and the "Click Song." This lateral is pronounced in the same way as hl, except that while breathing out, the voice is introduced.

The consonant sound Ng is pronounced like the last two letters in our word "sing." Where Ng is followed by a g [Ng'g], the second g is hard, as in "gun." The other consonant sounds are similar to those in English.

In these songs it has not been possible to show the variations in the vowel sounds of most Bantu languages. As a general rule, however, the vowels should be pronounced like those in Spanish, which have the following English equivalents:

A like the a in "father"
E like the ai in "bait"
I like the i in "machine"
O like the oa in "boat"
U like the oo in "boot"

A simple rule will be of help in pronouncing song titles: Place the accent on the next-to-the-last syllable ["Nom-thí-ni," "Khu-lú-ma"].

The Ballad Singer and Poetry-Making

The African singer, accompanied or unaccompanied, may sing or declaim a dramatic poem in an impersonal tone. The subject is often a tragic love story or a recital of death in battle. Frequently the traditional musician will use his instrument to compose poetry. To a foreigner the result appears merely as an integration of speech and rhythm. But to a person conversant with the language of the poem the result is profoundly beguiling. Rhythmic sounds from the instrument not only accompany the poet's words but spur him on toward ever more imaginative improvisations. He may muse on the uncertainties of life, quoting the misfortunes and successes of friends or well-known figures. To the accompaniment of a harp, he may narrate episodes from the history of his tribe. Since the attainment of political independence by various African countries, the emergence of political parties has not escaped the curious and roving fancy of the poet-musician. The victories or defeats of such parties have consequently been added to his repertoire.

Poetic Duets. Poetry improvisation with instrumental accompaniment attains its greatest success in contests between two musicians. In this particular form the two poet-musicians improvise upon the same topic with the same musical accompaniment. One recites a verse, whereupon the other adds a complementary verse, maintaining the same musical beat. Their topic may be love, war, tribal disasters, or any other important event.

The Poet-Musician and a Group of Singers. To the accompaniment of a musical instrument, usually a harp, the poet-musician may declaim or sing a verse while a group of singers, or his audience, sings a refrain to his poem. The topic may, again, be love or war, or else poverty or wealth, disaster or success, and, of course, current or historical events.

Love Poems. Musicians all over Africa improvise love poems to the accompaniment of a harp. A poet-musician may narrate verse at great length idolizing his love and extolling her beauty. In Western Uganda this type of poem assumes a stereotyped pattern of three parts. In the first part the narrator sets the scene, describing the place where he met his love. He also describes her beauty in great detail. Without delay he accosts her and proposes marriage. The proposal is immediately rejected. The second part is melancholic. He is unable to speak, eat, or drink. His parents, relatives, and friends are concerned. He attempts suicide. The third part is full of excitement, laughter, and jubilation because at last his love has been fulfilled.

The African Epic. This is a long narrative poem, recited immediately after a chorus of singers has performed; it is cultivated by the Cushite Bantu of Western Uganda, Rwanda, and Burundi,

as well as by the Xhosa, Zulu, Sotho, Venda, and Tsonga of South Africa. The words of the song have no bearing upon the ensuing poem, which is usually narrated by an old man of the village or community. The poem is generally composed around a hero who represents the ideal of an entire cultural epoch. Every effort is made to build up the image of the hero. He is the descendant of a whole line of heroes. He is a favorite of the gods. All his heroic deeds are quoted—as are some of his own words. In spite of the usual repetitions, this type of poem is dignified and exalted. Most of these epics are very old and have been handed down orally, while others are new and contain sentiments belonging to recent cultural epochs.

Song Texts. In most forms of African songs, words play a significant part. Indeed, it is usually the words that generate the music of the songs because most of the languages of the songs are musically accented. Both singers and audience listen for the meaning of the words of the song, which often convey a message. It is to be expected therefore that the greatest African traditional musician is also the greatest poet, historian, and storyteller in his part of the country.

Oral History of the African Song. When the Wanyamwezi of Tanzania, the Luo of Kenya, and the Bakiga of Uganda, to mention only a few, sing their long unending songs, they are in fact relating stories of historical interest. Here the musician fills the vacuum created by the lack of literature and the general illiteracy still existing in most of Africa. Thus the African folk song serves as an important repository of history, poetry, and tradition in general.

Part Singing in Responsorial Style

Part songs are not uncommon in Africa. The prototype of two-part singing is the responsorial style in which the solo enters before the end of the chorus part with a free contrapuntal tune.

In some songs, solo and chorus sing different contrapuntal melodies at the same time, with the chorus always maintaining an ostinato type of melody. Musical progression is maintained by the solo part with its variations and adventures into new pitches in free counterpoint with the ostinato chorus. The ostinato chorus may be in multi-parts, in which case we hear more than two parts.

The Two-Part Responsorial Form of Song. In this common form of song the two parts are performed by a soloist and a chorus of singers. The solo part is both interesting and difficult. The chorus merely repeats the same refrain throughout the song. The soloist, on the other hand, must be an expert musician. He bears the burden of singing the entire unwritten text of the song. Melodically his part undergoes several variations, whereas the chorus sings the same melody. At times he is called upon to enter before the chorus part ends, so that the two parts run together in free counterpoint.

Responsorial Style in Three-Part Form. This type of song is more advanced than the two-part. The soloist's part is onerous. Not only is he expected to sing the entire unwritten text, but he also in effect assumes the role of conductor of chorus and instruments. The music consists of a two-part responsorial form repeated after another contrasting two-part responsorial form, thus representing an A-B-A formula.

The Canonic Type of Part Singing. The canonic style of singing is common among the Giriama and some of the Luhya tribes of Kenya. The music is very advanced from the folk-song medium and cannot be sung without a conductor.

Form

We have already noted that African music in general is highly functional, and that, indeed, there is no social function that is not served by music. While it is beyond the scope of this Introduction to analyze in detail the forms of a variety of functional songs, an example of form may be cited. Among the Baganda of Uganda the installation of the heir to a public figure is an intricate ritual consisting of music, dance, and feasting. Songs for the occasion consist of long and often interesting texts. Musically, the responsorial form of this kind of song is cast into two contrasting

parts of the text, thus forming an A-B formula.

The story song is too vast a subject to treat here—to analyze the forms of story songs of even a single tribe would occupy volumes. We have noted that ballads and stories of all kinds are sung in a declamatory style by African musicians. In addition to this declamatory style, there are song stories in which the tune and words are of equal importance. Such songs are usually long and the musical form is complex. This type of song is common among the Giriama and Luo in Kenya, the Wanyamwezi in Tanzania, and the Bakiga in Uganda.

Rhythm in the African Song

What is true of the form of the African song is equally true of its rhythm—the subject is too vast to be treated here. We will only mention that a single song is multi-rhythmic. It consists of the rhythmic flow of singing, of hand-clapping, and of drums. The drums by themselves would be multi-rhythmic—as would be the singers in the case of songs sung in parts.

Within the same song there may be a change in the regularly recurring accented beat, thus causing a change of time signature. There are of course numerous odd-time signatures that are rare in European music, except in the contemporary style.

Musical Scale of the African Song

On this subject again there exists a wealth of material. Here it will suffice to say that there are songs of five-note scales, six-note scales, and seven-note scales within the range of one note and its equivalent above. Each of these scales appears in songs in different modes.

Tonality

In several monophonic songs there appear sequential repetitions, some of which are of complete melodies. Such repetitions may appear at intervals as great as a major third. They create an overall change of the tonality of the song. In several cases there are restatements of the melodies in their original tonality—a procedure which can be expressed in the formula A-A$_I$-A, where A is the melody, A$_I$ is the same melody at a different pitch, and A is the same melody at the original pitch. These are examples of complete and smooth modulation from one tonal center to another, with complete melodic change. This progression occurs particularly in a number of story songs.

All peoples, we are told, love that which is familiar to them. It is my hope that, as South Africa's music becomes better known, it will cease to appear alien or strange and instead form a cultural link between the peoples of Southern Africa and the rest of the world.

SOLOMON MBABI-KATANA

24

Performance Notes

We have tried to keep in mind a number of goals in transcribing and arranging these songs. Foremost has been that of simplicity. Therefore, precise accuracy in transcription has sometimes had to give way to playability. The songs have been arranged in keys easily applicable to both the piano and the guitar. In addition to metronome markings to suggest tempo, we have included individual rhythm patterns for both the guitar and the piano. Please use them only as suggestions. If you feel that embellishment will be tasteful, do not hesitate to modify. For example, the rhythm pattern for "Khuluma"

might be modified to something like this:

A few other suggestions...

For piano. Most of the songs have a definite "punch." Play *briskly,* except where noted. Use the pedal sparingly. Usually the rhythms have a definite staccato feeling, so in addition to a sharp attack, try to move crisply between bass and treble, punctuating the abrupt movement back and forth.

For guitar. Use "taps" extensively. This is done by either knocking the side of the thumb sharply against the top of the guitar just above and in front of the sound hole, or slapping the top with the fingers. Different "thump" qualities will result as you tap various places on the top. Normally the strings are stopped at the same time with the right hand, thereby arresting the sound. Down-and-up markings also suggest technique, and, where appropriate, right-hand fingerings are marked.

General suggestions. For clarity and inflection, listen to the recordings of Miss Makeba. [A discography is provided on page 119.] Learn to sing the melodies accurately. Some are challenging at first, especially those which employ non-chordal tones. If you take some time to reach perfection, you'll find the resulting harmony pleasantly rewarding. Often Miss Makeba chooses harmonies which seem to sidestep our traditional common ones. She often sings, for example, minor thirds against major chords in the accompaniment. Flatted sevenths are extensively employed, and accompaniment harmony is sometimes delightfully inconsistent. Try, for example, substituting II m 7 for II 7 in "Jikele' Maweni," without particular regard for regularity.

Don't hesitate to improvise. Bear in mind that these songs are normally highly individual in character, and are rarely performed the same way twice.

Thanks to Steve Steinberg, Demetri Pappas, and most of all to Anne Stoddard for their help with the arrangements. These were done so that you may find a different, challenging, and enlightening experience ahead. Welcome to the world of African song.

E. J. M.
J. G.

Qongqothwane

Qongqothwane

[The Click Song] . . . . .

The click song is a folk song of nonsense such as "Peter Piper picked a peck of pickled peppers." The song attempts to bring together as many click sounds as possible. It is based upon the Xhosan proverb: "Don't look down upon the Qongqothwane"—the knocking beetle from which the word derives its sounds. The earth-beetle is capable of revolving the top part of its body to point in any direction. The little children who play in the vast expanses of the Transkei (the original land of the Xhosa Kingdom, including the rest of Eastern Cape Province) have many songs about the different types of creatures who roam the Transkei. When playing in the fields, the young ones sometimes lift the little earth-beetle onto their hands and sing, "Beetle, beetle, which way is my home?" Then the beetle points in one direction or another. This beetle has become a philosophical guide in hardships; in moments of trouble or sadness someone will say, "Brace yourself, and the earth-beetle will point the way to a better future for you."

The doctor of the road is the beetle.
The doctor of the road is the beetle.
The doctor of the road is the beetle.
He climbed past this way,
They say it is the beetle.
He climbed past this way,
They say it is the beetle.
He climbed past this way,
They say it is the beetle.
He climbed past this way,
Oh! It is the beetle.
The doctor of the road is the beetle.

The bass line should sound like a flowing, independent part of the accompaniment. Strangely enough, it is reminiscent of early rock-and-roll in America.

♩ = 100

I - GQI - RA   LEN - DLE-LA __   NGU - QO NGQO-THWA-NE   I - GQI -

RA   LEN - DLE-LA __   NGU - QO   NGQO - THWA - NE

SE- BE-QA-BE-LE GQI THA - PHA BA - THI NGU - QO NGQO-THWA - NE

SE- BE- QA - BE - LE GQI THA - PHA BA - THI NGU - QO NGQO-THWA-NE

Zenizenabo

[Bring Them with You or Be Victorious]

A Xhosa war chant about the old tribal feuds.

This song is best left unaccompanied, but two additional harmony parts for voices have been transcribed. Though it looks difficult, each part is merely one restated phrase. Notice the challenging harmonies when the third part enters.

Bring them with you,
You idealistic cowards.
Bring them with you,
You idealistic cowards.
You cherish high ideals.
[These five lines are sung seven times.]
Hit, man, hit,
Son of my father, hmm, hmm, hmm, ho—o
Ho-hmm, son of my father,
Hit hard, man, hit.
Son of my father,
Hit hard, son of my father,
Hit hard.
As for your idealism,
Hey, ho, hey, ho, hey, ho,
Son of my father.

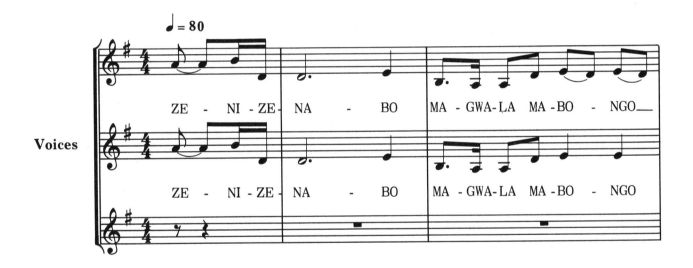

MA - GWA-LA MA -BO - NGO__ MA - BO - NGWE - NTLI - ZI - YO ZE - NI - ZE -

MA - GWA-LA MA -BO - NGO MA - BO - NGWE - NTLI - ZI - YO ZE - NI - ZE -

NA - BO MA - GWA-LA MA -BO - NGO__ MA -BO - NGWE - NTLI - ZI - YO ZE - NI - ZE -

QU - LA - MFO - NDI - NI QU - LA - MFO - NDI - NI - KA BA -WO_____

NA - BO MA - GWA-LA MA -BO - NGO__ MA -BO - NGWE - NTLI - ZI - YO ZE - NI - ZE -

QU - LA - MFO - NDI - NI QU - LA - MFO - NDI - NI - KA BA WO_____

NA - BO   MA - GWA-LA MA-BO - NGO___

A - HOM HOM   HO - HM___   HO - O

HE LE HO HE HA LA   HE LE HO

MA - BO -NGWE - NTLI-ZI -YO   ZE -NI -ZE-NA - BO

HO - HM___   KA - BA - WO___   QU - LA -

HE HA LA___ MA-BO - NGO HOM   HE LE HO

MA - GWA-LA MA BO - NGO___   MA - BO -NGWE - NTLI-ZI -YO___

MFO - NDI -NI   QU-LA -   MFO - NDI -NI   KA - BA-WO___

HE HA LA   HE LE HO HE HA LA___ MA-BO -NGO HOM

Ntyilo-Ntyilo

Ntyilo-Ntyilo

[Bird Song]

A lullaby-lament. A canary is singing, and though
the song is soft and beautiful melodically,
its words carry a sorrowful message: the African
no longer controls his own land.

I heard a sound from the bush.
I looked up, I drew near.
The sound I heard was
Ti, li, ti, li, ti, li.
Ntyilo, Ntyilo, Ntyilo.
That melody was beautiful.
I heard a voice from the bush.
I looked up, I drew near.
The voice said:
"There is trouble in the land."
Tra-la-tra-la.
That melody was beautiful.
The owner of the voice
Was dressed in white robes.
The owner of the voice
Was dressed in red robes.
The words were
Tra-la, tra-la, tra-la.
The melody was beautiful.

Play the song in a simple ballad style, softly
and delicately.

Um Home

[Song of Praise]

This is a Xhosa dance song of a patriotic nature whose words literally mean:

In her arrangement, Miss Makeba uses a string bass, which plays the same figure throughout the song.

> I praise my fathers who came from Ngoni *
> I am speaking for all my loved ones
> Let him alone to perform his dance.

* Bantu group

Moderately slow, blues type, sad

(Rhythm)   *(Voice)*

SENG - DZI - NGA — NEM -

HO _____ ME HE-LA-BA - BE _____

BA - TSHING - LE - LE NGO - NI _____ NI JI - YA — HOM —

YA-ZE YA -NGI - NYUN _____ DZE - LA - LEM -PE - KE - LE TE - LE JI —

— YA HO -MM— E -LA BA -BE ___ JI - YA HO-MM HO -MM   HO - OHO - OHO HO __ OHM —

JIYA - YIYA ___ I - O - OH OHM   HAYI - YA ___ OHO -HM - HO -HM

Ngoma Kurila

Ngoma Kurila

[A Lament]

A Venda lament. A mother's child cries from hunger, and she tries to comfort it.

A song without a particular key stressed and with a very hollow harmonic structure. On the piano, try playing the figure with a repetitive, drone-like quality.

On the guitar, keep a steady rhythm with a modified "G" chord:

The first section [in 4/4] should be sung *ad lib* and unaccompanied. In Africa, the usual accompaniment is played by a small thumb piano, known as a "mbira," and a bass cowbell.

Oh Mother! Oh Mother!
What am I going to eat today?
My child! I will prepare some food.
Dear Mother! Do so.

Jikele' Maweni

[Go Round to the Rocks]

This "Retreat Song" is a Xhosa warrior's cry of
defeat in battle. Contrast the meaning with the light
presentation and the parallels with war "games"
as indicated by the words. They describe
sham fights among boys, an ancient tradition
designed to instill bravery.

Use a flowing, heavy rhythm and watch the
accents. The first eight measures are unaccompanied and should have a definite *ad lib*
feeling, though the metronome marking and
time signatures have been provided. Use
them as a rough guide.

The boys' sticks will come to life at the river
  Yo Homm!
When sticks knock against one another
  I yo Homm!
Men are afraid of going to the river
  Yo Homm!
Because sticks are knocking one against the other.
  I yo Homm!

Go round to the rocks,
We are going soon.
[These two lines are sung four times.]

The boys are dancing.
They dance beautifully.
The boys are dancing,
They dance to celebrate
Their departure for the mines.
[These five lines are sung twice.]

Go round to the rocks,
We are going soon.
[These two lines are sung four times.]

The men met,
It was beautiful.
The men met,
They met for the trip to the mines.
They met and it was beautiful.

Jikele' Maweni

I - NTO NGA ZA MA KWEN-KWE ZO VU KE LEM-LA - NJE NI YO HOMM

XA KU BE - THI - NTO NGA I YO___ HOMM A MA DO DA YO YI - KA

U - KU BE KEM - LA___ NJE NI YO HOMM KU - BA KU BE - THI - NTO NGA I YO___ HOMM A-

JI - KE - LE' MA - WE - NI SI - YA HA - MBA JI - KE - LE' MA - WE - NI SI - YA

HA - MBA___ JI - KE - LE' MA - WE - NI SI - YA HA - MBA

JI - KE - LE' MA - WE - NI SI - YA HA - MBA___ A XHEN - TSA - MA KWEN - KWE A

INTO YAM

INTO YAM

[My Man]

A literal translation of "into yam" would be "my thing," but in this love song it means "my man." In Xhosa society, drinking is not regarded as an evil, but drunkenness is. Hence this woman is eager to explain why she loves her man in spite of his drunken habits. She and her mother do not see eye to eye on this point. She is quite satisfied with her man as he is.

I love my man.
Though he drinks
And gets drunk,
I love him very much.
He works for me.
When I left home,
I was good.
When I lived in Johannesburg *
I became spoiled.
My man, Mother!
Is my own.
My own man,
My own man, Mother!
It is my man.
Oh, keep quiet, Mother!
Keep quiet, Mother,
Keep quiet, Mother.
My man,
I love him.
Though he drinks
And gets drunk,
I love him very much.
He works for me.
My man, I love him.
Though he drinks liquor.
Oh, I love him very much.
He works for me,
My man.
You are denying me my man,
You are denying me my man,
You are denying me my man,
You are denying me my man, Mother.

* Johannesburg-e Goli

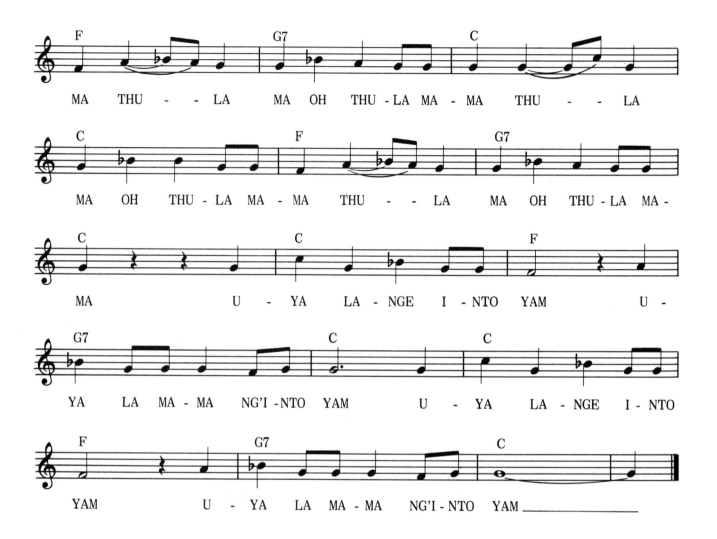

Dubula

Dubula

[Shoot]

This is a Xhosa folk song performed during the course of a particular tale. Note the allusion in the third line, and the social context in the preparation of the young warrior.

The suggested rhythm pattern is rhythmically strict, but try modifications such as reversing the bass notes or syncopating the second and fourth beats.

Oh, bird of song,
What are you carrying
In your beak?
I am carrying
Curdled milk for my young, father!
Why do you carry
Milk that is not yet ready?
Oh, oh, hmm.
Shoot, boy! Shoot, boy!
Shoot with that rifle.
Take care!
Shoot, boy! Shoot, boy!
Shoot with that rifle.
Take care
Lest you burn *
Shoot, boy,
Shoot with that rifle.
Shoot, boy!
Take care!
Lest you burn.
Hey, hey, shoot, shoot!
Hey, hey, shoot, shoot!
Hey, hey, shoot, shoot!
Be careful lest you burn.

* Burn refers to a powder burn from the misfiring of an old-fashioned gun.

Nomthini

[A Girl's Name]

Try doubling up the time in your accompaniment.

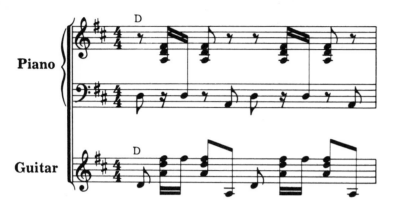

Beyond those mountains,
Lives a beautiful maiden.
Beyond those cliffs,
Lives a beautiful maiden.
Beyond those mountains,
Lives a beautiful maiden.
Beyond those cliffs,
Lives a beautiful maiden.
They say her name is Nomthini.
They say her name is Nomthini.
They say her name is Nomthini.
They say her name is Nomthini.
No other maiden is like her.
No other beauty is like her.
No other maiden is like her.
No other beauty is like her.
If only I had wings,
I would fly there.
If only I had wings,
I would fly there.
I would see her while she is still alive.
I would see her while she is still alive.

Nomthini

Magwalandini

Magwalandini

[You Cowards]

Since no man likes to be regarded as a coward, this reference to cowardliness is used as a patriotic challenge to rouse men to action.

This arrangement of the 3/4 rhythm is a bit tricky for guitar. Be sure to include all beats.

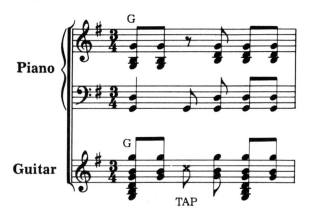

Look out, you cowards!
Time passes by, you cowards!
Look out, you cowards!
Time passes by, you cowards!
Why do you sleep,
You cowards?
Why do you sleep,
You cowards?
Why do you sleep?
You cowards?
Why do you sleep,
You cowards?
You cowards!
You cowards!
You cowards!
You cowards!

Amampondo

[Pondo Man]

A song describing the brave Pondo people, their courage and alertness.

Pay special attention to the accent on the third beat. The guitar might play a "tap."

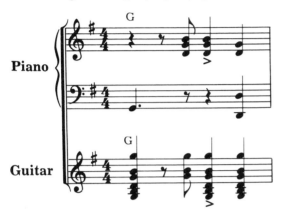

They were here,
The Pondos.
They rose early.
They were here,
The Pondos.
In their sleep
They hummed.
Ho-humm
Ho-humm
Ho-humm
In their sleep
They hummed
Ho-humm, hmm,
Father, homm,
Ho, ho, hmm.
They were here,

The Pondos.
They rose early.
They were here,
The Pondos,
They rose early.
In their sleep
They hummed.
Hmm, hmm,
Father, ho, hmm
Ho-hmm
They hummed
Ho-hmm
Ho-ho-hmm
Hm, Father, ho, hmm
Ho-hmm!

A - BE -LA - PH'A - MAM - PON - DO   A - YA -VU - KE   KU - SEN

A - BE -LA - PH'A - MAM -PON - DO BA - BO   HI - YO VU - KE   KU - SEN

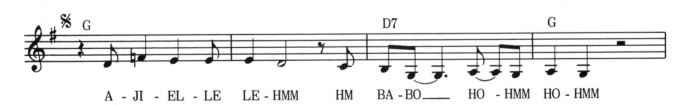

A - JI - EL - LE   LE - HMM   HM BA - BO____ HO - HMM HO - HMM

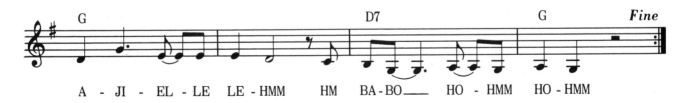

A - JI - EL - LE   LE - HMM   HM BA - BO____ HO - HMM HO - HMM

A - BE -LA - PH'A - MAM - PON - DO   A - YA - VU - KE   KU - SEN

Woza

[Come]

A Zulu lament with a definite American blues-like quality. A young urban couple try to overlook their difficulties and find joy in the future.

Make full use of the blues possibilities in this song by accenting offbeats and stressing seventh chords.

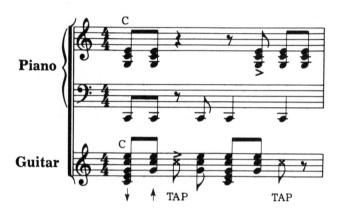

Come, love,
Let us live happily.
Come, my love,
Let us live happily.
Look at our troubles!
Mother and father
Are in tears. Oh, Mother!
For long we have tried
To say "Come back to me,"
But I do not know
What is the problem. Oh!
We have tried this,
And we have tried that,
To make it clear
The loved one is mine.
But all the time
She is not moved. Oh!
Come, love,
Let us live happily.
In happiness, Oh!
I am happy
When I am with you.

Maduna

Maduna

[Maduna Clan]

"Maduna"—tormentor of young girls. This is the
story of a woman's courage in a face-to-face
encounter. A Xhosa song written by Miss Makeba.

Fie, do not look at me, you maduna,
What will you do to me?
Fie, do not look at me, you maduna.
What will you do to me?
You are insignificant, you maduna.
What will you do to me? Oh, me!
Why! Fie, you are insignificant, you maduna,
What will you do to me?
Fie, do not look at me, you maduna.
What will you do to me?
No, maduna, you are insignificant.
What will you do to me? Oh, me!
Do not look at me, you maduna.
What will you do to me? Oh, me!
Never again will you disturb me.
Never again will you disturb me.
You have disturbed me far too long.
Far too long you have made things difficult for me.
You have disturbed me far too long.
Far too long you have made things difficult for me.
Welele! maduna,
What will you do to me?
Welele! maduna,
What will you do to me?

Use a swinging, syncopated rhythm, almost
Latin American in flavor.

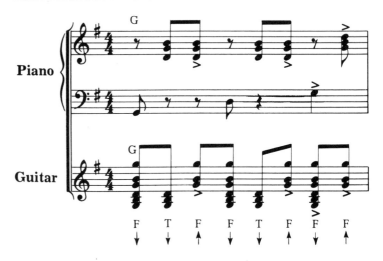

Qhude

Qhude

[The Cock]

In early Xhosa communities, the cock's shrill crowing in the morning roused all sleepers to meet the new day. One of the first duties of a daughter-in-law was to rise at dawn, before any other member of the family was up, and fetch water from the nearest river or spring—usually some distance away from the household.

The theme of this song is the awakening of the daughter-in-law [Makoti] to fetch water for the household. It is called "Qhude" because the song does the work of the Qhude or cock by rousing her.

A heavy, almost ponderous rhythm. Be sure to accent the second half of the first beat, and watch the triplets in the voice.

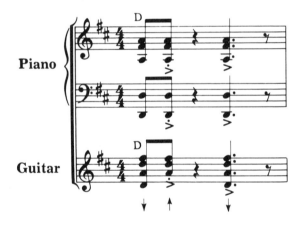

Wake up, daughter-in-law,
It is morning, oh, Mother!
There are sounds at the rocks,* oh, Mother!
Proclaiming the day, the water, O Cock!
There are sounds at the rocks, oh, Mother!
Proclaiming the day, there is no water!
Awake, there is no water!
Awake, daughter-in-law, there is no water!
Awake, daughter-in-law, there is no water!
Awake, daughter-in-law, there is no water!
They proclaim at the rocks!
It is morning, oh, the Cocks!
They proclaim at the rocks, oh, Mother!
It is morning, there is no water,
There is no water, there is no water, there is no water.

* In Xhosa folklore, "rocks" usually refers to rocks found in or near a river.

Umqokozo

[A String of Beads]

A Xhosa folk song performed at parties and feasts.

Note the ascending bass line.

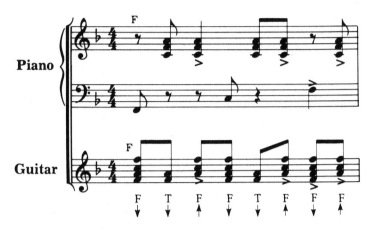

I have a string of red beads.
It was given to me
By my father.
[These three lines are sung three times.]
I have a string of red beads, Mother, hey!
They say, hey, Mother,
I have a string of red beads, Mother, hey!
They say, he, le, le,
The children are crying.
They cry, he, le, le,
I have a string of red beads,
Mother, le, le, le.
I have a string of red beads.
It was given to me
By my father.
[These three lines are sung three times.]
I have a string of red beads.

Umqokozo

CAMEROON

"What a beautiful country, Cameroon . . ."
Miss Makeba learned this song from Dorothy
Masuka while visiting Kenya. The lyrics are Zulu,
added by Miss Makeba.

Oh! Oh! Oh! Cameroon,
My home is in the Cameroons.
Oh! Oh! Oh! Cameroon,
I am going back to the Cameroons, Mother,
Oh! Oh! Oh!
Cameroon, Mother!
Oh! Oh! Oh!
Cameroon, Mother!
Oh! Oh! Oh!
Cameroon, Mother!
Rooni, Mother!
Cameroon, Mother!
Cameroon.

Here the accents are on the downbeats. Keep the
bass line flowing and accent the "taps"
on the guitar.

Cameroon

Uyadela

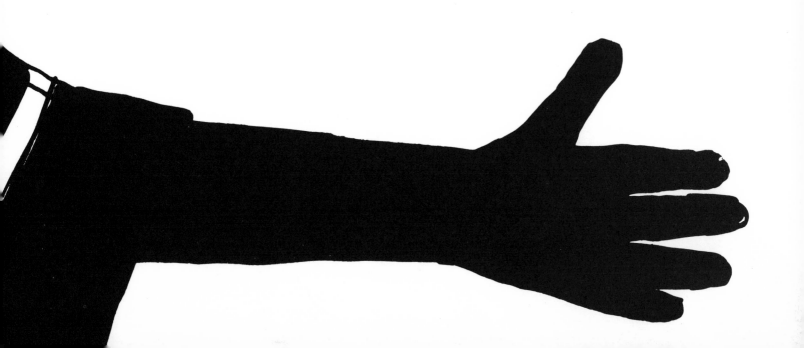

Uyadela

[You Are Arrogant]

A warning to a friend not to give up so easily. The rock rabbit is missing a tail because he had resigned himself to not receiving one. When the rest of the animals went to fetch their tails, he alone was unfortunate. The words are Zulu.

You are arrogant!
You are arrogant!
You are arrogant!
Because you like others to do things for you.
You are arrogant!
You are arrogant!
You are arrogant!
Because you like others to do things for you.
They say the rock rabbit has no tail,
Because it liked others to do things for it.
Oh, Ma-Mntambo, you are arrogant.
You are arrogant,
Because you like others to do things for you.
You are arrogant.

Make sure you include the last half of the fourth beat.

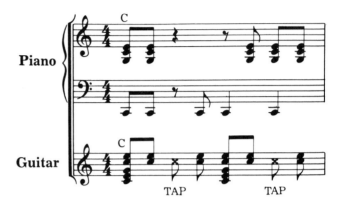

Mayibuye

[Restore Africa to Its Owners]

This is a Xhosa song which tells of the resentment of South Africa's young generation to the government in power. It is a patriotic song, and one of several African folk songs important for their oral history. Following is a literal translation:

We true South Africans have suffered for a long
    time
As a result of white people laws.
Awake, my people.
The time for our liberation has come.
This land is ours.
Remember Kings Umshoeshoe, Dingaan,
Umzilikazi, and Ngqika.
They fought for this land.
Awake, ye Africans,
Remember the words of King Shaka
Which he spoke on the arrival of white people.
"Do not trust the white man,
Because he has come to take your land."
Oh, my Father! Unite my people
I beg you, let's fight for our land.
We have long been ruled by the Dutch,
We have long suffered under their rule.
The time for your liberation has come.
The whole of Africa is ready to fight for our
    freedom.
You Zulu, Xhosa, Shangane, Basuto, Venda unite.
There is no more time for crying.
Restore Africa right now.

Follow the road of our forefathers
And fight for our land
Which was taken by white people.
We want our liberation now.
Beware, my people.
Awake Mandela and Sisule,
Sobukwe and you Luthuli, Tambo, Nokwe, and
    Resha.
Awake, ye Africans.
Remember the words of Ngqika,
"Do not trust the white man,
Because he has come to take your land."
Oh my Father! Unite my people
I beg you, let's fight for our land.
We have long been ruled by the Dutch,
We have long suffered under their rule.
The time for your liberation has come.
The whole of Africa is ready to fight for our
    freedom.
You Zulu, Xhosa, Shangane, Basuto, Venda unite.
There is no more time for crying.

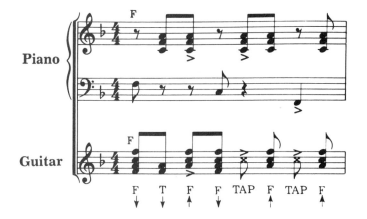

Mayibuye

Bajabula Bonke

[I Became III]

In this song, a man laments his fate of getting
sick and thus bringing joy to many who envy him.
Impaka is a mythical, cat-like animal used by
witch doctors for casting an evil spell on people.
This is the "poisonous dish" which the woman
served to her husband.

My father, how they rejoiced over my illness!
They danced, hmm, hmm.
Hey, they rejoiced over my illness,
They danced, hmm, hmm.
I became ill.
I was confined to my bed.
I became ill.
I was confined to my bed.
I became ill.
I was confined to my bed.
Hey! They danced because of my illness.
They danced.
Oh, hmm!
Hey! My!
My dearest one
Prepared a poisonous dish for me.
Hmm! Hmm! Hey! Father.
I became ill. My, I became ill,
I was confined to my bed.
I became ill and lay on my bed.
I lay on my bed. Oh! I was confined to bed.

Slow and unaccompanied. Each note should
be heavy and ponderous.

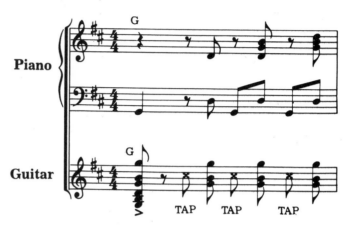

Bajabula Bonke

Olilili

Olilili

[Lullaby]

A very slow lullaby-lament. A woman quiets her hungry child. Once again, the feeling of the song is *ad lib,* but the metronome marking and time signatures are included as a guide. Miss Makeba presents the song in patterns alternating with the chorus, as marked.

Accompaniment should be nonrhythmic and should simply identify each chord as it appears.

Early one morning,
In the homelands,
On my way
To my favorite haunt
In the homelands,
I heard a beautiful voice
From the hilltop.
It was a haunting melody
In the homelands.
The woman sang beautifully
In the homelands.
Her voice was beautiful,
Beautiful over the hills.
Oli-li-li, A lu-lu-lu, Oli-li-li,
Oli-li-li, A lu-lu-lu, Oli-li-li.
Sleep, my baby, I am lulling you to sleep.
Do not cry, my baby, I am comforting you.
Sleep, my baby, I am lulling you to sleep.
Do not cry, my baby, I am comforting you.

♪ = 96

Solo NGE - NYI MI - NI E - KU SE NI_____ Cho. E - MA KHA YE NI

Solo NDA - NDI SI - NGE E - BO - NGWE - NI_____ Cho. E - MA KHA YE NI NDE Solo

VA NGE ZWI - E - LI - I - MMA - NDI Cho. LI - MMA NDI NGA PHE - ZO KO - LU - NDI

Solo LA - TSHO KA - SI - THU - KU THE - ZI_____ Cho. E - MA KHA YE NI

Solo WAN TJI LO - ZA KE - LOM - FA - ZI_____ Cho. E - MA KHA YE NI E

TSHO NGE ZWI E LI - I - MMA - NDI LI - MMA NDI NGA PHE - ZO KO - LU - NDI

(Cho.) O - LI - LI - LI A - LU - LU O - LI - LU - LU LA - LA SA - NA - NDI YA - KU

BA - NDE ZE - LA_____ THU - LA - SA - NA - NDI YA - KU THU - THU ZE - LA_____

Cho. O - LI - LI - LI A - LU - LU O - LI - LU - LU_____

NOMEVA

NOMEVA

[The Wasp]

This is a story in song. In the first stanza, a man and his wife are bickering. As a result, their baby is neglected and cries, wanders off to a prickly pear bush, and injures himself on the thorns. The mother is so agitated that she is not in a fit and proper state to suckle her baby. The man admits his guilt to some unknown deed; he says his sin has found him out. Nomeva is the Xhosa word for "wasp," and there are "stings" in all three stanzas. The woman is stung in the first stanza by her uselessness and ugliness; the baby is stung by the thorns in the second stanza; the man is stung by his sin in the third.

The first section is *ad lib* and unaccompanied. Keep the rhythm simple, and accent the third beat.

Of what use are you?
You are so ugly.
What can I do?
You are so ugly.
Do you see them
Strutting proudly?
Do you see them, oh, doctor, oh yes?

The child is crying.
Thorns are pricking him.
Those are not thorns,
It is the prickly pear.
My, this child loves you.
In the cliffs
The young are given suck.

I do not mind what happens now,
My sin has found me out.
I do not care what happens.
My sin has found me out.
Oh_____!
Oh_____Mother!
Oh! Oh! Oh!
[The last two lines are sung twice.]

LANGA MORE

Langa More

[More Sun]

There is a great deal of excitement in this
song. The people have learned a new type of dance
and they enjoy it immensely. They call this new
dance "feast of the feet." They feel so light
on their feet, they imagine themselves able to
jump to the sun.

Tap, tap, oh, more sun.
Tap, tap, oh, more sun, hey, hey, hey.
You are teaching us, come in and see
The feast of the feet, hey, hey, hey.
It makes us move, come in and see
The feast of the feet. We are walking, mmh!
We are gathering, we shall pat each other, oh!
We are going to be mad.
We are walking, hmm, we are gathering.
We shall pat each other, oh!
We are going to be mad,
We are going to hit the sun.
[This line is sung three times.]
We are going to hit the sun more, hey, hey, hey,
   hey.
You are teaching us, come in and see
The feast of the feet, hey, hey, hey, hey,
It causes us to move,
Come in and see the feast of the feet.
We are going to hit the sun more,
We are going to hit the sun, hmm, hmm.

Watch the staccato rhythm.

108

Thanayi

Thanayi

[No, Child]

In this song, two girls are mentioned—Nomalizo and Nomalungelo. Muntu is their husband. Nomalizo is pining away because Nomalungelo is pregnant and she is not. Muntu's mother imagines all kinds of things her son may be doing at the mines. She consoles Nomalizo and tells her not to consider death as the answer to her childlessness [which the Xhosa consider lack of achievement].

"Thana" is a term of endearment meaning "child." "Thanayi," when fully written, would be "thana hayi."

What can the matter be, Nomalizo, ohmn?
What can the matter be, Nomalizo, ohmn?
Nomalungelo has put on so much weight.
The navel has sunk.
If you have achieved nothing on earth
You are better off dead.
No, child, no.
No, child, no,
Child, no, child, no, child, no.
[Repeat the above verse once.]

I can imagine my child
Sitting in the mines,
Muntu!
What can the matter be, Nomalizo? Ohm, no,
I can imagine my child
Playing at being grown-up.
What can be the matter, Nomalizo, Ohmn?
What can be the matter, Nomalizo, Ohmn?

Try using a drone bass note for the first eight measures,

then break into this bright rhythm, with special emphasis on the "taps" for guitar.

Khuluma

[Speak]

A sorrowful tale of poverty in the townships. "Khuluma," written by Betty Khoza, tells of an unwanted visitor who is rebuffed by a woman whose husband has not yet returned from his job in the city. When he does return, he addresses the prowler in the words of the song.

Say, man, say, the sun has set
In my absence, what is it
You would be seeking in my homestead?
Say, man, say, the sun has set
In my absence, what is it
You would be seeking in my homestead?

The household sleeps.
Make no entrance.

Though elsewhere you may have succeeded
In this sort of thing,
Here you may not dare!

Be sure to watch the placing of the staccato marks.

Khuluma

Index of First Lines

Discography

The Voice of Africa—Miriam Makeba
[RCA Stereo LSP 2845]

> Nomthini
> Langa More
> Qhude
> Mayibuye
> Uyadela

The World of Miriam Makeba
[RCA Stereo LSP 2750]

> Dubula
> Um Home
> Amampondo
> Into Yam

Miriam Makeba
[RCA Stereo LSP 2267]

> Jikele' Maweni
> The Click Song [Qongqothwane]
> Um Home
> Olilili
> Nomeva

Makeba Sings!
[RCA Stereo LSP 3321]

> Cameroon
> Woza
> Khuluma
> Maduna

The Many Voices of Miriam Makeba
[Kapp Stereo KS 3274]

> Zenizenabo
> Ntyilo-Ntyilo
> Umqokozo
> Ngoma Kurila
> Thanayi
> Ngagula [Bajabula Bonke]